VOLUME 6
MAELSTROM

AQUAMAN

VOLUME 6
MAELSTROM

AQUAMAN

WRITTEN BY
JEFF PARKER

PENCILS BY
PAUL PELLETIER
CARLOS RODRIGUEZ
ALVARO MARTINEZ
DANIEL HDR

INKS BY
SEAN PARSONS
SANDRA HOPE
WAYNE FAUCHER
RAUL FERNANDEZ
BIT
DANIEL HDR
TONY KORDOS
RICK MAGYAR

COLOR BY
RAIN BEREDO
PETE PANTAZIS
GUY MAJOR

LETTERS BY
DEZI SIENTY
TAYLOR ESPOSITO
CARLOS M. MANGUAL
TRAVIS LANHAM
DAVE SHARPE

COLLECTION COVER ART BY
PAUL PELLETIER
and SEAN PARSONS

AQUAMAN CREATED BY
PAUL NORRIS

AQUAMAN VOLUME 6: MAELSTROM

Published by DC Comics. Compilation and all new material Copyright © 2016 DC Comics. All Rights Reserved.

Originally published in single magazine form in AQUAMAN 32-40, SECRET ORIGINS 2, 5 Copyright © 2014, 2015 DC Comics.
All Rights Reserved. All characters, their distinctive likenesses and related elements featured in this publication are trademarks
of DC Comics. The stories, characters and incidents featured in this publication are entirely fictional.
DC Comics does not read or accept unsolicited ideas, stories or artwork.

DC Comics, 2900 W. Alameda Ave., Burbank, CA 91505
Printed by RR Donnelley, Salem, VA, USA. 1/29/16. First Printing.
ISBN: 978-1-4012-6096-5

Library of Congress Cataloging-in-Publication Data

Parker, Jeff, 1966- author.
Aquaman. Volume 6, Maelstrom / Jeff Parker, writer ; Paul Pelletier, artist.
pages cm. -- (The New 52!)
ISBN 978-1-4012-6096-5
1. Graphic novels. I. Pelletier, Paul, 1970- illustrator. II. Title. III. Title: Maelstrom.

PN6728.A68P37 2014
741.5'973--dc23

IT'S TIME I CAME TO *SEE* YOU.

TO FINISH THE JOURNEY YOU BEGAN ALL THOSE YEARS AGO, DURING THE STORM OF THE CENTURY.

YOU SAW THE *LIGHTHOUSE KEEPER* LEAVE HIS POST TO GO TO A SINKING SHIP.

YOU'D SEEN OTHER MEN FROM LAND, BUT NONE SO HEROIC.

IN A MOMENT, THE SITUATION REVERSED, AND *TOM CURRY* WAS NOW THE ONE WHO NEEDED HELP.

HE COULDN'T HAVE IMAGINED ANYONE BEING THERE FOR HIM...

...MUCH LESS MEETING HIS *SOUL MATE* IN THE SEA.

THE TIME YOU STAYED ON LAND WAS THE HAPPIEST TOM HAD EVER KNOWN.

I HEAR I WAS PRETTY HAPPY TOO.

BUT TOM, THIS IS MY LIFE'S WORK--WE *AGREED*--!

HE'S NOT FEELING WELL-- SORRY, DOCTOR. GOOD TO MEET YOU, MISS.

ARTHUR, *PLEASE!*

UH... WOW--

STEPHEN-- IT'S TOO S-- IT'S *NOT TRUE!*

CAN'T...I PROMISED HER...

NO, ARTHUR. IT'S STILL...TOO SOON. GET OUT OF AMNESTY FOR A FEW DAYS.

THE ISLAND TRIP IS SOON--I COULD HELP DANNY WITH HIS PRACTICE RUN...

DO THAT. I HAVE TO TAKE CARE OF SOMETHING AT HOME.

WHAT HE TOOK CARE OF WAS A *MINI-LAB* SHIN HAD SET UP IN THE BASEMENT. DAD HAD MADE HIM AGREE TO KEEP HIS FINDINGS THERE, INSTEAD OF THE OCEANOGRAPHIC INSTITUTE.

AN AVERAGE ATLANTEAN WOULD BE RESISTANT TO PRESSURE, BUT UNLIKELY TO BE AS STRONG AS WHAT ARTHUR EXHIBITS.

I POSTULATE THAT THIS IS DUE TO THE REINTRODUCTION OF SPECIALIZED GENES, SEPARATED BY THOUSANDS OF YEARS OF EVOLUTION.

AS FOR THE ABILITY TO COMMUNE WITH AQUATIC SPECIES...

SHIN AND THE REPORTER ARRIVED IN TIME TO SEE DAD SEND ALL THAT RESEARCH INTO THE OCEAN.

I WENT OUT TO HELP DANNY.

WAKE UP, DANNY--YOU MADE A GOOD CATCH!

SORRY TO TAKE THE FUN PART, COULDN'T WAIT TO SEE HOW THE HAUL WENT.

YEAH, WELL, ONLY *YOU* COULD HAVE DONE THAT, ART.

HA... HUH?

THE *HOIST* ISN'T WORKING YET, WHICH MEANS YOU PULLED THAT *TON* OF FISH UP *YOURSELF.*

AND I KNOW YOUR SKIFF NEVER HAS GAS IN IT, YOU DRAG IT OUT FOR LOOKS. "SWIMMING."

HA! COME ON MAN, YOU'RE STILL DREAMING...

ART, I'M NOT *STUPID.* I *KNOW* YOU'RE NOT LIKE THE REST OF US.

THE FISHERMEN IN MY FAMILY TOLD *STORIES* ABOUT SEA PEOPLE.

PEOPLE LIKE *YOU.*

MAYDAY, MAYDAY! AN AIRPLANE HAS GONE DOWN OFF POINT RAY--

WHERE IS HE?!

I WANT A NAME!!!

SEVEN BELLS

I WOULDN'T HEAR ANYTHING THAT WOULD SLOW ME DOWN.

I FOUND THE RIGHT VESSEL...

YOU KILLED HIM! WHY! WHY?!?

AAHH--

KRAKKKK

...AND THE WRONG MAN.

DAD...?

BACK IN TOWN, THE REPORT SAID MY FATHER HAD CONTRACTED PNEUMONIA, AND THE INFECTION HAD SPREAD TO HIS HEART. THE THIEF HADN'T DONE ANYTHING VIOLENT--THE EXCITEMENT TRIGGERED THE CARDIAC EPISODE.

THE SON WAS A CAREER CRIMINAL LIKE HIS FATHER. HE WOULDN'T BE REPORTING ME. INSTEAD, HE'D DEDICATE THE REST OF HIS LIFE TO RETURNING THAT PAIN IN KIND...

...AS THE BLACK MANTA.

GRADUATION

JEFF PARKER: WRITER   ALVARO MARTINEZ: PENCILLER   RAUL FERNANDEZ: INKER
RAIN BEREDO: COLORS   DAVE SHARPE: LETTERS

BUT HER **REAL** TARGET WON'T BE **EMPTY ARMOR** CONTROLLED BY HER **FATHER**.

I SHOULD BE THE ONE TO DO THIS, MY KING!

NEREUS, YOU ARE A GREAT WARRIOR, BUT BOLDNESS WILL ONLY TAKE YOU SO FAR. MERA IS THE PERFECT CHOICE.

WEAPON-LESS, SHE WILL BE WELCOMED IN ATLANTIS AS A NOMAD.

AND THEN, UNSEEN, SHE'LL **KILL THE KING OF ATLANTIS!**

XEBEL WILL HAVE STRUCK BACK AT THOSE THAT **EXILED** US.

BY TRADITION, MERA AND I ARE **BETROTHED.** THE ROYAL FAMILY ALWAYS JOINS WITH THE MILITARY CHIEF.

YOU MADE OUR **PACT!**

ONCE I BECOME ROYALTY THE WATER-SHAPING POWER WILL PASS TO **ME,** AND I **CAN** COMPLETE THE MISSION.

EVEN IF I PASSED MY CROWN ON TO YOU NOW, IT WOULD TAKE YOU YEARS TO LEARN TO MOVE THE WATER LIKE MERA.

THIS WHOLE PLAN SEEMS DESIGNED TO KEEP HER **AWAY** FROM ME, MY KING!

LET MY DAUGHTER **PASS.**

NOW, MERA--FULL SPEED, PUSH YOUR SLIPSTREAM TO THE SMALLEST POINT BEFORE YOU...

...GO!

I WILL MAKE YOU PROUD!

YOU... ALWAYS... HAVE.

WHOOOMM

SIRE! WHAT'S HAPPENED?!

I...I WILL BE FINE. IT WAS...NOT EASY.

MUST... REST. YOU NEARLY TOOK THE MANTLE JUST NOW, NEREUS.

I CAN'T DESCRIBE THE MOMENT I SURFACE FOR THE FIRST TIME.

JEFF PARKER writer PAUL PELLETIER penciler SEAN PARSONS RICK MAGYAR (PGS. 40, 44) inkers RAIN BEREDO colorist DEZI SIENTY letterer
PELLETIER, PARSONS and BEREDO cover art

DR. SHIN, WHAT'S THE NATURE OF THE EMERGENCY?

HAS LAB 9 BEEN *INFILTRATED?*

OPEN HATCH-- PASSCODE ZETA!

ORSON'S *EXPERIMENT*-- HE'S MADE SOMETHING *DEADLY!*

THERE-- THERE WAS NOTHING WE COULD DO--

STAND BACK.

YOU TWO, CLEAR THE DOORWAY.

SSSHHHHHSSHK

ORSON USED THE *BODY* OF THE DIVER, *COOMBS...*

...AND *PARTS* FROM EVERY CREATURE HE'S STUDIED! HE WAS REACHING DOWN INTO THE TANK WHEN--

--GET *BACK,* I SAW IT MOVE!

I DON'T SEE ANYTHING-- COULD IT HAVE GOTTEN OUT?

WHAT. THE HELL.

HAPPENED.

SKKKRRRSH

NICE CRAB-DRIVING, TULA.

IT'S NOT MY SPECIALTY, BUT I GET BY.

SO I'M *DONE* HEARING THE USUAL SLURS ABOUT WHERE I'M FROM AND BLAH BLAH BLAH.

I WANT TO KNOW EVERYONE ACTIVE IN YOUR GROUP AND HOW IT IS ORGANIZED.

NNNHHHRRR...

KILL ME. I WILL TELL YOU *NOTHING!*

YOU AND YOUR MATE WILL DESTROY ATLANTIS ANYWAY, I WILL ONLY DIE SOONER.

IT'S NOT ABOUT *WHETHER* YOU WILL DIE, TRAITOR.

IT'S ABOUT *HOW.*

 "YOU'RE IN LUCK."

FEW OUTSIDE OF COURT GET TO WITNESS THIS. *TOPO'S FEEDING TIME.*

IT'S NOT A *QUICK* THING, THE WAY HE EATS. HE TENDS TO SWALLOW AND LET HIS CATCH SLOWLY DIGEST.

THIS-- THIS IS--

DISCOVER THE MYSTERIES OF HIS MANY STOMACHS. YOUR MEN WILL FOLLOW UNTIL I FIND OUT EVERYTHING.

I WILL TELL YOU OF OUR SECT!

WHAT DO YOU WANT TO KNOW?!

TOPO *IS* AN INSPIRING SIGHT.

ONE CAN'T ARGUE WITH RESULTS.

STRANGE.

YOU'RE UP OUT OF YOUR DEPTH FOR A COLOSSAL SQUID.

WONDER IF YOU'RE SICK, OR THERE ISN'T ANY--

WHAT--! I WASN'T THREATENING...

-:HHHK:- STOP!

THAT'S-- ENOUGH--

BACK... OFF.

DON'T GET IT--

--HEAR ME!

DOESN'T MAKE ANY SENSE, SHE DIDN'T RESPOND!

IS SOMETHING INTERFERING WITH MY--

--AHHHH!

WHAT THE HELL--

WHAT'S MAKING YOU ALL DO THIS--?!

STOP!

WHEEERRRRE...

...DID YOU GOOOO...

THE NORTH SENTRY WAS RIGHT, IT *IS* THE KING!

SIRE-- ARE YOU ALL RIGHT?

THE ANIMALS--THEY *ATTACKED* YOU--WHAT HAPPENED?

THAT...MAY TAKE SOME TIME TO ANSWER.

WHAT'S THE NEWS IN ATLANTIS?

ALL ANYONE SPEAKS OF IS THE QUEEN'S MISSION!

MISSION? *MERA?*

SHE AND CAPTAIN TULA CAPTURED AN ENTIRE SECT OF CONSPIRATORS!

THEY ARE IN THE PRISON COVES!

WHAT...?

YOU MEAN SHE DIDN'T *TELL* YOU...

FINALLY.

I HEAR *YOU'VE BEEN BUSY.*

GOOD *TIMING, MY KING...*

...HISTORICALLY, INSURRECTION IN ATLANTIS HAS TO BE DEALT WITH *SWIFTLY.*

AND *HARSHLY.*

I PLAN TO-- AFTER I LOOK INTO A *NEW* PROBLEM.

KAE, CAN YOU SUMMON THE ELDER OF SCIENCE FOR ME?

AT ONCE.

SIRE, AS THE ELDER OF LAW, I MUST ADVISE YOU THAT ASSASSINATION ATTEMPTS ARE THE MOST *GRAVE* TRANSGRESSION.

THE PENALTY... IS *EXECUTION.*

THAT DOESN'T--

RBBBRRRMMMBBRKRRLLL

SEAQUAKE!

EDRID ORSON, ENTRY 31-14. I HAVE NOW INTRODUCED THE CELL FUSION FROM MY ALTERED SUBJECTS TO CREATE THE CAMOUFLAGE DEFENSES.

STONE FISH. MIMIC OCTOPUS. LEAF SCORPIONFISH. ALL THE MOST *ADAPTIVE* CORAL.

ADDED TO THE NERVOUS SYSTEM OF A HUMAN, OUR CHIMERA WILL SURPASS ALL THE DONORS IN STEALTH ABILITY.

HNNRR... RRGGHH...

THOUGH AN *EXTREME* CAMOUFLAGE COULD BE...

...PAINFUL.

YOU! HANDS BEHIND YOUR HEAD!

SLURRRGHH

SSLRGGHHH

FOUND HIM, DISPATCH. SOME NUT IN A COSTUME, LOOKS LIKE--

SIR, THIS IS *NOT* A NUDE BEACH! IF YOU DON'T PUT CLOTHES ON, YOU *WILL* BE ARRESTED--

YES. CLOTHES.

HOW-- MY GOD--

--HOW ARE YOU *DOING* THAT?

SSHHLLRRKK

SKKLLCCHH

HHHHHH--

WHERE'S *ANDY?* ONE SECOND, HE WAS ON THE RADIO, AND THEN...

SOUNDED LIKE THEY SHOULD HAVE CALLED *ANIMAL CONTROL*--

CAMOUFLAGE.

"IT COULD EXERT ITS WILL THROUGH THE SEA CREATURES... LIKE YOU?"

ROWR--RROOWR!!!

HSSS!!

SALTY, NO!

SO SORRY SIR, HE'S NOT USUALLY LIKE THIS--!

RRRRLLL!!!

--GOT IT, I'M HEADING OVER THERE NOW--WHOA!

Specials
Venti Parker $2.89
Grande Pelletier $3.15
Mocha ... oy $3.04
Perry-... chord $3.29
Cacner ... ons $2.79
Rain...

ERIKA-- OH GOSH, NOW WE'RE CATCHING EVERYBODY!

C'MON, SALTY, CALM DOWN!

THIS DAY IS AWFUL, JENNY. ONE OF OURS-- ANDY--WAS FOUND DEAD DOWN AT SOUTH BEACH.

LIKE HE HAD BEEN SHOT--MULTIPLE TIMES. THEN JUST AS I'M HEADING OUT THERE, GUESS WHO CALLS?

ARTHUR. HE SAYS DR. SHIN HAS BEEN LIFE- FLIGHTED TO A NAVAL HOSPITAL SHIP OFF BOSTON.

OH GOD, IS HE GOING TO BE OKAY?

ARTHUR.

YOU SAID HE *CALLLLED YOOOUUU.*

AAH!!!

BAAB'S BOOKS

HOW CAN HE STILL BE--

AAAAGHH--!

I NEED TO *KNOOOW,* ERIKAAAA...

WHERE-- *THERE!*

HE IS BACK, I CAN SENSE HIM!

HEADING TO...

...BOSTON.

BOSTON HARBOR. MEDICAL SHIP "HAVEN."

I CAN'T BELIEVE IT. ARTHUR?

HOW DID YOU KNOW I WAS HERE?

WHAT GOOD IS BEING A KING IF I CAN'T HAVE SPIES CHECKING UP ON...WELL, POTENTIAL THREATS.

ESPECIALLY AT TRITON BASE. I KNOW NOW IT'S AN INTERNATIONAL EFFORT, LIKE THE SPACE STATION.

I ALSO KNOW ABOUT CHIMERA-- THAT'S WHAT HURT YOU, ISN'T IT?

YES. YOU'VE SEEN IT?

IT ATTACKED ME... REMOTELY.

"IT'S INCREDIBLY DANGEROUS. ARTHUR, YOU MUST TELL ME EVERYTHING ABOUT YOUR ENCOUNTER..."

FROM THE FILES I READ, ORSON HAD COMBINED EVERY BREAKTHROUGH WITH AQUATIC LIFE INTO THIS PROJECT.

THE BIG UNKNOWN WAS HOW THE *BRAIN* WOULD FUNCTION. HE USED THE *KARAQAN* TISSUE BECAUSE IT WAS PERFECT FOR THE PURPOSE.

"BUT WOULD THE CHIMERA THINK MORE LIKE THE KARAQAN... OR LIKE THE DIVER YOU RESCUED?

"OR SOME HYBRID OF BOTH? DR. ORSON NEVER INTENDED TO FIND OUT, AS HE BUILT A CEREBRAL UNIT TO *CONTROL* THE CREATURE'S MIND...

" ... BUT IT KILLED HIM BEFORE HE COULD IMPLANT IT. HOWEVER ITS MIND WORKS, IT MUST HAVE MEMORIES OF YOU SAVING *AND* DESTROYING IT, ARTHUR...

"...MAKING *YOU* THE PIVOTAL FIGURE IN ITS EXISTENCE. CHIMERA IS *DRIVEN* TO SEEK YOU OUT."

WHAT DO YOU THINK MADE US BOTH *BLACK OUT?*

IT HAD GREATER ABILITY WITH AQUATIC LIFE--IT ASSUMED ITS MIND WAS MORE POWERFUL THAN YOURS.

BUT THE KARAQAN ANSWERED TO YOUR ANCESTOR. IT'S LIKELY A GENETIC CONFLICT.

I COULD UNDERSTAND IT BETTER IF I HAD MORE ATLANTEAN HISTORICAL RECORDS, BUT I KNOW THAT'S IMPOSSIBLE.

THOSE... CAN'T BE MOVED. BUT THERE'S SOMEONE I WANT YOU TO MEET WHEN YOU'RE MORE RECOVERED.

I'LL CHECK IN AGAIN SOON.

NO ONE ADMITTED WITHOUT CAPTAIN'S ORDERS!

I HAVE TO DELIVER A MESSAGE TO DOCTOR SHIN. IT WON'T TAKE LONG.

DR. SHIN NEEDS *REST.*

I UNDERSTAND, KING.

ARTHUR... THAT'S *COOMBS,* THE DIVER!

LAND AND SEA

JEFF PARKER writer CARLOS RODRIGUEZ penciller BIT inker RAIN BEREDO colorist DEZI SIENTY letterer PELLETIER, PARSONS and BEREDO cover art

HSSSSSSRRRLLL...

ARTHUR! COVER YOUR FACE!

HRRLRLLLLHH...

HRLOORGH!!!

AAAAH!!

WHKRRRRSSHH

AGHH!

I SHOULD HAVE SUMMONED THE ANIMALS TO BE READY FOR YOU.

DOESN'T MATTER...

I AM ALL OCEAN LIFE.

BITE THAT.

WHROAAAHR!!

KRAAH--

THAT'S A GREAT IDEA, COOMBS.

KLANG

THOLOM

"HOW LONG HAVE I LIVED IN THE DARK?

"I HAD ALL THESE QUESTIONS, EVEN AS A BOY. HAD I FORGOTTEN THEM ALL?

"I GOT A FEW ANSWERS. THERE WAS A WORLD BELOW I WAS CONNECTED TO.

"MORE THAN CONNECTED, I WAS ITS KING.

"STORYBOOK ANSWERS. THEY FELT FINAL, SO I QUIT ASKING THE QUESTIONS.

"I THOUGHT THERE WAS NOTHING MORE TO FIND.

"AND NOW FINDING NOTHING WOULD CHANGE EVERYTHING..."

--LEASE RETURN OUR CALLS, DR. SHIN. MR. BLYTHE IS ADAMANT YOU RETURN TO YOUR WORK AT TRITON BASE AS SOON AS YOU ARE ABLE.

WE UNDERSTAND IT WAS A TRAUMATIC EXPERIENCE, BUT--

CLICK

REPLAY VIDEO MESSAGE.

STEPHEN, LOOK AT MY BIG GRADUATE!

SORRY YOU COULDN'T BE HERE, UNCLE. HOPE YOU CAN COME OUT TO SAN FRANCISCO SOON!

DR. SHIN?

EH?

I'M EBERLIN FROM TRITON BASE. YOU HAVEN'T BEEN RETURNING OUR CALLS.

I WAS ALMOST KILLED DOWN THERE. HAVE SOME DECENCY...

SIR, YOU KNOW A LOT OF CONFIDENTIAL INFORMATION ABOUT TRITON.

YOU CAN'T JUST WALK AWAY FROM US.

WHAR-RARH

WHOA! *WHOA!*

DR. SHIN, IS THIS MAN BOTHERING YOU?

DOWN, SALTY.

IN FACT, HE IS!

I WAS JUST TRYING TO DISCUSS WORK...

SIR, ACCOSTING CITIZENS IN AMNESTY IS WORTH *JAIL TIME.*

WE'LL BE IN TOUCH SOON, DR. SHIN.

LET US GIVE YOU A RIDE, DOCTOR.

THANK YOU VERY MUCH, LADIES. I'M AFRAID HIS PEOPLE WON'T BE PUT OFF FOR MUCH LONGER.

I DON'T THINK YOU'LL HAVE TO WORRY ABOUT WHOEVER THEY ARE.

WE'RE ACTUALLY BRINGING YOU DOWN TO THE PIER UPON *REQUEST.*

REQUEST? WHO SENT YOU?

AN OLD FRIEND OF OURS...EVEN IF YOU TWO HAVE HAD SOME TOUGH TIMES.

THERE HE IS-- THEY FOUND A PLACE TO DOCK!

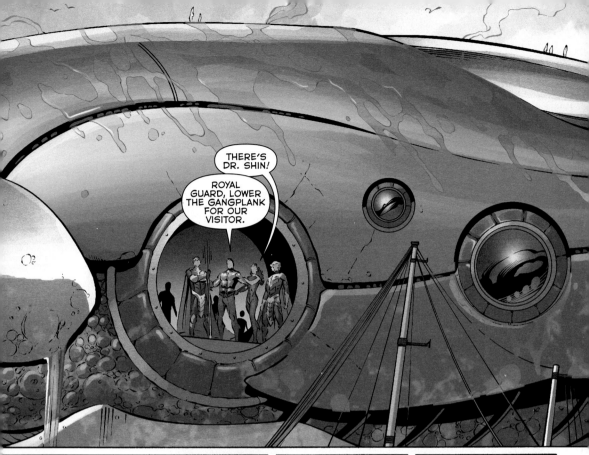

THERE'S DR. SHIN!

ROYAL GUARD, LOWER THE GANGPLANK FOR OUR VISITOR.

NO, YOU'RE ON OUR VERSION OF AIR FORCE ONE. I SENT TULA'S GUARD TO RETRIEVE THE BOOKS AND FILES YOU'LL WANT TO TAKE.

THERE'S SOMEONE *ELSE* COMING DOWN WITH US. I DON'T KNOW IF YOU'VE MET HIM BEFORE.

IT'S AN HONOR, DR. SHIN. I'VE READ EVERYTHING YOU'VE EVER PUBLISHED.

LIKEWISE.

GOOD, BECAUSE YOU TWO ARE GOING TO BE WORKING TOGETHER CLOSELY.

YOU'LL HAVE ACCESS TO ALL THE ARCHIVES OF ATLANTIS.

YOU CAN'T BE...REALLY? WHY?

ATLANTEANS ARE TOO REVERENT OF OUR HISTORY TO *QUESTION* IT.

I NEED YOUR INPUT TO FIGURE OUT HOW IT ALL REALLY WORKS. AND *WHY...?* ATLANTIS IS TEARING ITSELF APART-- BECAUSE OF *ME.*

SEAQUAKE!

RIGHT ON SCHEDULE.

WE HAVE TO GO HELP! THERE WILL BE DAMAGE!

YOU SEE THE PROBLEM, SCHOLARS.

IF ARTHUR HAS FAITH IN YOU, SO DO I.

OUR GLORIOUS KING HAS RETURNED.

THAT'S RIGHT, UNDER-REALMER.

IT ALSO MEANS THAT TOMORROW, *TRAITORS* TO THE KINGDOM PAY THE *PRICE*.

BUT YOUR MORE *DIRECT CRIMES* ARE KILLING HONORED MEMBERS OF THE ROYAL GUARD, AND THE ATTEMPTED ASSASSINATION OF OUR QUEEN.

THE COUNCIL OF ELDERS HAS GIVEN THEIR DECISION TO ME AFTER MUCH DELIBERATION.

THEY DECREE THAT IN THE TRADITION OF ATLANTIS, ALL CONSPIRATORS AGAINST THE REALM... FACE *EXECUTION.*

STILL, THIS IS A MONARCHY, AND HERE *I* RULE.

I DON'T LIKE GOING AGAINST THE COUNCIL, BUT I ALSO THINK *THEY* DIDN'T LIKE HAVING TO MAKE THIS CALL.

AGAINST THE WIDE WORLD, ATLANTIS IS A SMALL NATION.

THERE ARE TOO FEW OF US TO ERASE *DOZENS,* EVEN IF THEY ARE TRAITORS TO THE REALM.

INSTEAD, I AM *EXILING* YOU. YOU WILL BE TAKEN TO A POINT I'VE FOUND NEAR ANTARCTICA.

IT HAS A DEEP CHASM WITH A LAVA VENT, SUSTAINING MORE THAN ENOUGH FOOD SOURCES.

THIS TRANSPORT VESSEL WILL THEN BE *SUNK* SO YOU CAN USE IT AS QUARTERS WHILE YOU BUILD YOUR NEW COLONY.

SIRE, I WOULD LIKE TO POINT OUT THAT THIS IS ROUGHLY HOW THE ENEMY NATION OF *XEBEL* WAS CREATED.

AND WE HAVE LOST THE KNOWLEDGE OF HOW TO CREATE A BARRIER AS WITH THAT COLONY.

TRUE, ELDER KOAH.

BUT THAT BARRIER KEPT THEM ANGRY WITH US LONG AFTER ANYONE COULD EVEN REMEMBER WHAT THE ORIGINAL DISPUTE *WAS*.

BUT... YOU'LL STILL EXPECT US TO FOLLOW YOUR LAWS!

NO. YOU CAN PRACTICE WHATEVER YOU WANT. IT'S YOUR COUNTRY.

VOW ETERNAL VENGEANCE, KNOCK YOURSELF OUT.

BUT YOU'VE GOT A CHANCE TO STOP BEING DEFINED BY *FEARS* AND DO SOMETHING *MORE*.

I KNOW YOU DESPISE SURFACE PEOPLE, THOUGH YOU'VE NEVER MET ANY. LOOK UP.

THEY *COULD* STAY ON THE LAND, BUT THEY MOVE OUT OF THEIR ELEMENT TO EXPAND. TO *GROW*.

ARE YOU ANY LESS CAPABLE?

A WAY TO STOP THE QUAKES?

FOR NOW, YOU COULD STAY OUTSIDE THE MIDDLE PERIMETER--IT BEGINS AT THE ARMORY.

BUT WE HAVE A PROBLEM BASED ON HOW ATLANTIS SENSES.

SENSES?

THIS IS ACCEPTED AS MAGIC; I THINK IT'S ARCANE *SCIENCE.* BUT THE SUNKEN CONTINENT ISN'T LIKE ANY OTHER LAND MASS ON EARTH.

WHEN ATLANTEANS DIE, THEIR ELECTRICAL IMPULSES--AND ALL THEY KNOW--ARE ABSORBED INTO THE STRATA. BECOMING PART OF A *SYSTEM.*

THIS IS HOW CERTAIN FUNCTIONS AND SAFE-GUARDS ARE PASSED ON--A MAJOR ONE BEING THAT NO SURFACE MAN CAN RULE, OR ATLANTIS WILL TEAR ITSELF *APART.*

I'M ONLY HALF...

WHICH MITIGATES THE EFFECT OR ATLANTIS WOULD HAVE SHAKEN TO RUBBLE BY NOW.

YOUR ATLANTEAN HALF BEING SIRED BY A ROYAL SHOULD OVERRULE IT COMPLETELY.

THERE'S THE DILEMMA. YOU ARE KING BY THE LAST QUEEN'S PASSING. BUT...

...ATLANTIS ITSELF DOESN'T *RECOGNIZE* THAT STATUS, ARTHUR.

HIS MIND IS CLEAR. HE BELIEVES THE STORY HE TELLS. IT'S WHAT HE SAW.

I FIGURED THIS COULDN'T BE THAT EASY.

AN... ALIEN?

TO THE REST OF THIS WORLD, *YOU* SEEM ALIEN, SIR.

I AM ADOPTING YOUR DORSAL GILLS TO ADAPT.

J'ONN J'ONZZ IS FROM MARS.

AND A TELEPATH--THE PERFECT PERSON TO HELP FIGURE OUT WHAT REALLY HAPPENED THAT DAY.

TULA, PLEASE TAKE VULKO TO THE NAUTILA THEATRE. WE'LL BE THERE SOON.

YOU CAN ALSO TELL ME WHAT'S *BOTHERING* YOU, I KNOW THAT LOOK FROM MERA.

IF I CAN SPEAK FREELY?

THIS IS THE *THIRD* OUTSIDER YOU'VE BROUGHT IN, AND THE FIRST TWO HAVE *ALREADY* TURNED OUR WORLD UPSIDE DOWN.

HE IS *FAR* MORE DANGEROUS. I BELIEVE THEY CALL HIM THE MARTIAN *MANHUNTER*.

"ORVAX MADE MANY *ENEMIES* IN HIS THIRTEEN YEARS AS KING, AND ONE OF THEM FINALLY *REACHED* HIM.

"IT WAS ORM'S TWELFTH BIRTHDAY, WHICH WOULD HAVE BEEN HIS *MERITUNIS*--THE CELEBRATION OF ADOLESCENT ASCENSION.

"ATLANNA DECIDED TO HAVE HIS CEREMONY A FEW DAYS LATER, ANYWAY--ROYALS ALWAYS USE THE THEATRE-- WITH ENTERTAINMENT AND A BANQUET.

"SHE HAD THE CITY ACTORS PERFORM ORM'S FAVORITE HISTORICAL PLAY.

"ONLY I KNEW THAT SHE PLANNED TO LEAVE ATLANTIS *AGAIN*, NOW WITH *ORM*. MY LOYALTY WAS TO *HER*.

"I ARRANGED PASSAGE TO THE SURFACE, WHERE THEY WOULD BE IMPOSSIBLE TO FIND.

"IT WAS THE PERFECT CHANCE. THE WHOLE REALM WOULD STAY UP LATE, WITH LIBATIONS AND EXCESS.

"THE QUEEN AND PRINCE WOULD MEET MY DRIVER IN THE MIDDLE OF THE NIGHT."

"AND THEN THE PLAN WAS WIPED AWAY IN A BREATH.

"A PROP THAT SHOULD HAVE MADE A BRILLIANT LUMINESCENT DISPLAY FOR THE FINALE *EXPLODED.*

BOOM

"THE ONLY PEOPLE IN THE REGAL BALCONY AT THE TIME WERE ATLANNA, ORM, AND ME. I WAS FORTUNATE.

"ATLANNA... WAS *NOT*. ORM MANAGED TO DODGE THE BURST..."

...ALMOST AS IF HE *EXPECTED*--

THAT'S ENOUGH, VULKO. NO SPECULATION.

OKAY, J'ONN. WHAT DO YOU NEED FROM US?

HIS RECOUNTING WAS ENOUGH. NOW I CAN HOME IN ON THE POINT.

IT'S INCREDIBLE.

SINCE I'VE ARRIVED, IT'S LIKE THE *WHOLE CITY* HUMS WITH THOUGHT... FEELING.

ANY SOLID PHYSICAL PLACE, LIKE THOSE FULL OF STONE, HOLDS IMPRESSIONS OF WHAT HAPPENED BEFORE.

"IN TIME, WE HAD THE REASONING POWER TO REALIZE WE WERE *MORE* THAN EQUALS.

"THEY STOPPED PROVIDING THE KELP, BUT IT WAS *TOO LATE.* IT WAS THE *SINGULARITY* OF 2,000 YEARS AGO.

"THEY DROVE OUR PEOPLE BACK INTO THE FORESTS, BUT THAT WAS NOT THEIR HOME ANYMORE.

"AND THE GORILLAS HAD NO CONCEPT OF ORGANIZED BATTLE.

"BUT SOMETIME LATER, WHEN AN ARMY TROOP *TRAVERSED* THE FOREST, THEY WERE BROUGHT DOWN--AND ONE APE RESOLVED TO SEND A MESSAGE BY MAKING A MEAL OF THEIR GENERAL.

"WHEN HE REACHED THE BRAIN, IT WAS REVELATION. HE HAD ABSORBED THE KNOWLEDGE OF HIS PREY. HE HAD DISCOVERED *CERESORBIS.*

"SOON WE HAD PLANS, *STRATEGIES.* WITH THE ALL THE KATANGALAN SECRETS CONSUMED, WE TOOK THE CITY."

MOST OF THE HAIRLESS FELL, A FEW ESCAPED THROUGH THE GATE.

IT'S AN OCEAN REALM!

NO...THIS ISN'T IT.

WE'RE IN THE PACIFIC OCEAN, UNDER SOME ISLAND.

LET'S LOOK ON THE SURFACE.

REMEMBER, ANCIENT ATLANTEANS DIDN'T BREATHE WATER, THAT GATE MUST HAVE *SUNK* AT SOME POINT.

LET'S TRY THESE GUYS. *MALO E LELE!*

< DO YOU KNOW OF...A CARVING? SOMETHING CALLED *MAELSTROM?* >

<I DON'T KNOW THAT WORD.>

MAELSTROM IS A SCANDINAVIAN WORD THAT TRACES BACK TO WHATEVER THE ATLANTEAN TERM WAS. THEY DON'T RECOGNIZE IT.

<HERE.>

⟨THIS?⟩

⟨YES! OTHER END OF ISLAND.⟩

⟨MANY THANKS. ALL THE FISH ARE GATHERED OVER IN THAT COVE OVER THERE.⟩

⟨THANK YOU! ?⟩

WHEN DID YOU PICK UP POLYNESIAN PHRASES?

I HUNG OUT IN THESE SEAS FOR A WHILE.

HEY.

THIS HAS TO BE WHAT THE FISHERMEN MEANT.

IT'S IMPRESSIVE, BUT DOESN'T LOOK ATLANTEAN.

THIS IS WHERE SHE WENT--IT *HAS* TO BE!

ARTHUR, STOP.

YOU'VE WAITED DECADES, DON'T RUSH NOW.

EXACTLY!

I'M NOT WAITING ANY LONGER!

CCRRKK

KRRAKK

MERA, LOOK! IN THE CENTER!

THIS IS THE ONE SHE *TOOK!*

ARTHUR!

SEE, NOW YOU'VE GOTTEN *MERA* MAD!

NOT-- PASS!

FIRE-- WEAK--

I THOUGHT PUTTING OUT THE FLAMES WOULD STOP THEM!

IT'S FIGHTING *NATURE*. WE'LL WEAR OUT BEFORE THEY DO.

THEY'RE HERE TO STOP ENEMIES FROM GETTING THROUGH!

FIGHTING THEM IS USELESS! WE HAVE TO REACH THE CENTER!

AND *THAT ONE* HAS THE TRIDENT!

IT'S HAPPENING!!

THEY'VE STOPPED...

BUT.... WHERE DOES THE GATE OPEN? I THOUGHT IT WOULD BE RIGHT HERE...

I FEEL IT...IT FEELS LIKE WHEN I PASSED THROUGH THE BARRIER OF XEBEL...

ARTHUR!

IT'S OVER HERE...IN THE SEA!

THIS WHOLE SECTION OF THE *ISLAND* IS THE GATE, AND THE *PORTAL*...

...IS THE *MAELSTROM.*

THE SAME PLACE...

NO, LOOK AT THE VOLCANO.

A VOLCANO IN THE SAME *PLACE*, BUT NOT DEAD AND DORMANT.

A FIXED POINT IN *TIME* THAT NEVER CHANGES...

IT *OPENED!* THE MAELSTROM GATE OPENED!

WITHOUT THE QUEEN'S ORDER?!

LOOK AT HIS BELT--THE CREST OF ATLANTIS!

THEY ARE ROYALS--THEY HAVE COME FOR YOU!

FEAR NOT, MY FAITHFUL. I KNEW THIS DAY WOULD COME.

I AM PREPARED.

MAELSTROM PART V: PACIFICA
JEFF PARKER writer PAUL PELLETIER penciller SANDRA HOPE, WAYNE FAUCHER inkers PETE PANTAZIS colorist TRAVIS LANHAM letterer
PELLETIER, PARSONS and BEREDO cover art

LIES!

AH!

...ORM CAN ONLY BE DEAD.

HHKKH--

YOU SHOULD HAVE TRIED POSING AS MY SON *ORM*.

I WOULD RECOGNIZE *HIM*, EVEN NOW. BUT SINCE ANOTHER WEARS THE CREST...

ATLANTIS HAS TAKEN MY FAMILY...MY FREEDOM.

MY FIRST CHILD AND TOM CURRY DIED LONG AGO, AT THE HANDS OF A HUSBAND I DIDN'T CHOOSE.

ORVAX *BOASTED* OF IT, THINKING I WOULD DROP MY PLANS TO LEAVE HIM.

INSTEAD, ON THAT DAY, I LEARNED I COULD *KILL*.

YOU GREW UP A NOMAD, LENU. YOU DON'T KNOW THE TREACHERY OF ATLANTEAN RULE.

THE COUNCIL WHO RESENT THE ROYALS.

THE MILITARY CHIEFS WHO HOPE TO MARRY *INTO* THAT ROYALTY AND TAKE OVER.

IT WAS ALWAYS THAT WAY. IN MY TIME MARRIED TO ORVAX MARIUS, I SOUGHT OUT LOST KNOWLEDGE THAT MIGHT HELP ME.

THAT'S HOW I LEARNED ABOUT THE *MAELSTROM*, AND HOW IT LED HERE.

TO *PACIFICA*.

THIS ARCHIPELAGO WAS TO BE A NEW HOME FOR THOSE WHO DIDN'T WANT TO EMBRACE LIFE BELOW THE WAVES, WHEN ATLANTIS WAS SLOWLY SINKING.

ANCIENTS SECRETLY CULTIVATED IT, STOCKED IT WITH THE ATLANTEAN BEASTS.

BUT ALL PEOPLE WERE TURNED BACK OR KILLED. ONLY *YOU* COULD FINISH WHAT THEY STARTED.

EVEN *I* WOULD HAVE FAILED HAD I NOT FOUND THE STAFF OF STORMS.

YOU CANNOT ESCAPE THE QUEEN! THE ISLANDS ANSWER TO HER!

SHE CAN FIND US ANYWHERE!

I DON'T *WANT* TO ESCAPE HER.

I WANT HER TO LISTEN TO ME. TO KNOW WHO I AM.

YOU'RE HER ADVISOR, YOU HAVE TO *MAKE* HER BELIEVE ME.

WHY SHOULD I?!

BECAUSE IT'S *TRUE*.

I BELIEVE SHE ALREADY KNOWS.

AND IT DOESN'T MATTER.

THEN YOU BELIEVE ME?

I'M NOT *BLIND.* YOU LOOK MORE LIKE HER THAN ANYONE I'VE EVER SEEN.

BUT I HAVE KNOWN ATLANNA FOR A LONG TIME NOW.

"ONCE SHE FOUND PACIFICA, SHE CAME BACK FOR MY KIND."

"THOSE WHO HELPED HER FIND THIS LOST LAND AND BURY ALL THE PATHS THAT WOULD LEAD TO IT."

THOSE WITH *PURPLE EYES.*

YES. WE ARE NOT ONE GROUP OR LINEAGE. PURPLE EYES CAN BE BORN ANYWHERE IN ATLANTIS.

WE HOLD ANCIENT SECRETS OF THE REALM.

"WE DON'T KNOW WHY WE ARE LIKE THIS. THE TRUTHS COME OUT WHEN A QUESTION IS PRESENTED TO US...LIKE AN ORACLE."

FOR YEARS THOSE LIKE ME WERE EXILED. SOME WENT TO THE SURFACE, MOST FOUND WILD TERRITORIES IN THE OCEAN.

ATLANNA FOUND AS MANY AS SHE COULD AND BROUGHT US HERE.

THEY ARE IN THE GLADE.

LENU!

AH!!

HOLD HIM!

GRRRR...

OFF!

WHERE ARE WE GOING?

I'M NOT FIGHTING MY MOM!

LET'S GET TO THE WATER AND REGROUP!

ARTHUR, THE MAELSTROM!

DID SHE ACTIVATE IT?

TULA! NEOL! WHAT ARE YOU DOING HERE!

IT IS OUR DUTY TO ASSIST--AND IT LOOKS LIKE YOU *NEED* IT!

PUT DOWN YOUR ARMS, I COMMAND YOU!

WHAT--?

THOSE FORCES ARE COMING TO KILL YOU!

THAT IS ATLANNA--MY *MOTHER!*

ARTHUR!

BOOM BOOM BOOM BOOM

I HATE TO BE THE ONE TO KEEP BREAKING BAD NEWS...

MAELSTROM PART VI: THE EDGE OF THE WORLD
JEFF PARKER writer PAUL PELLETIER penciller SANDRA HOPE, WAYNE FAUCHER, TONY KORDOS inkers RAIN BEREDO colorist TRAVIS LANHAM letterer
PELLETIER, HOPE and BEREDO cover art

KARAKU THE ELEMENTAL KEPT COMING UP IN WHAT WE FOUND ON PACIFICA.

HE'S WHY THE ATLANTEANS ORIGINALLY ABANDONED THIS SPACE AS A REFUGE-- BUT THE TABLETS DETAILING THAT WERE DESTROYED LONG AGO...

HER BEASTS ARE NO MATCH FOR HIM.

SIRE, WAS SHE NOT TRYING TO KILL YOU WHEN WE ARRIVED?

I DIDN'T COME ALL THIS WAY TO FIND ATLANNA JUST TO WATCH HER DIE!

AAAHHH!!

THE FIRE TROLLS FOLLOW THE WILL OF KARAKU.

THE ATLANTEANS BATTLED HIM LONG AGO, WHEN THE MAELSTROM WAS IN THE OTHER OCEAN.

OTHER OCEAN...?

THEY SENT A PROTECTOR TO ATTACK HIM. IT WAS RAISED FOR THAT PURPOSE. IT BROKE KARAKU, THOUGH HE SLOWLY FORMED AGAIN. WITHOUT HIM, THE FIRE TROLLS FELL.

THE KARAQAN!

YES. THE KARAQAN BURNED AND FELL IN THE NORTHERN SEAS...NEVER TO BE SEEN AGAIN.

HANG ON, DANIEL, THEY'LL HAVE FIRST AID IN THE SUB--

NOT... GOING TO... BE ENOUGH... ARTHUR...

...NOT NOW. AND YOU WON'T GET THROUGH THIS DAY...UNLESS YOU DO WHAT LENU SAID.

COMBINATION... OF WATER AND FORCE. HARDEN THE LAVA... BREAK THE HEAD OFF. YOU CAN DO IT...I'VE SEEN YOU GO.

I CAN'T LE--

I'M... ALREADY GONE. THANK YOU FOR LETTING ME GIVE...BACK.

I TOOK FROM YOU... DIDN'T DESERVE IT. AND YOU STILL GAVE ME THE GIFT OF A LIFETIME.

YOU BROUGHT ME...TO... ATLANTIS.

GOODBYE, MY FRIEND.

THE ATLANTEAN KING HAS DROPPED HIS GUARD. WILL YOU NOT HELP HIM?

YOU CANNOT PAUSE FOR OTHERS IN BATTLE.

HE WILL PAY THAT PRICE.

BOOM BOOM

BOOM BOOM BOOM

BOOM BOOM BOOM BOOM

MERA!!

TAKE...

...THAT.

I NEVER KNEW SUCH DEVOTION FROM MY OWN MATE.

AS YOU TO YOURS.

WHEN I REALIZED YOU MIGHT STILL BE ALIVE, NOTHING STOOD IN MY WAY OF TRYING TO FIND YOU.

ALL I HAD WAS A LIFETIME OF QUESTIONS. WHY HAD YOU LEFT? WHEN WOULD YOU COME BACK?

WHAT WERE YOU *LIKE?*

I THOUGHT ONLY OF THE YOUNG WOMAN WHO RAN OFF TO SEE ANOTHER WORLD... AND FELL IN LOVE.

NOT THE ONE WHO WAS TAKEN *AWAY* FROM IT. FORCED INTO A LIFE SHE HATED.

YOU'VE LIVED A WHOLE *OTHER* LIFE SINCE THEN...

...AND TO SURVIVE YOU HAD TO LEAVE THAT YOUNG WOMAN BEHIND.

YOU THINK I'D UNDERSTAND THAT. I DO, *NOW.*

I DON'T EXPECT ANYTHING OF YOU, ATLANNA.

KNOWING YOU'RE ALIVE IS ENOUGH.

WE'LL GO NOW.

THANK YOU.

THE TRIDENT!

AND THERE'S MORE...

ATLANNA'S ROYAL SIGNET?

THIS IS WHAT YOU WANT--A SHELL OF SOUNDS!

LIKE MY MOTHER LEFT FOR ME.

I'VE NEVER USED ONE OF THESE...

JUST TRY TO TOUCH IT...WITH YOUR MIND. PROJECT THAT YOU'RE READY TO LISTEN.

ARTHUR, YOU'VE LEFT SOMETHING BEHIND. MORE PROOF THAT YOU ARE WHO YOU CLAIM. NO PURE ATLANTEAN ROYAL WOULD HAVE BEEN ABLE TO PART WITH HIS TRIDENT.

YET YOU SEEM TO KNOW THERE IS MORE TO THE WORLD THAN ARTIFACTS.

THE END

START AT THE BEGINNING!

AQUAMAN

VOLUME 1: THE TRENCH
GEOFF JOHNS and IVAN REIS

AQUAMAN VOL. 2: THE OTHERS

AQUAMAN VOL. 3: THE THRONE OF ATLANTIS

JUSTICE LEAGUE VOL. 3: THE THRONE OF ATLANTIS